NdjenFerno

NdjenFerno

Lindsay Hill

Vatic Hum Press

Acknowledgments

Thanks is expressed to the editors of the following publications where these works, sometimes in earlier versions, first appeared:

Caliban NdjenFerno, Socket

Central Park Prophecy

Juxta The Method Of Steepest Descents (both), Holders, From The Cutout box

New Orleans Review What My Father Said In The Underworld (knots)

Orpheus Grid He Wire, Two Books, Wheel

River City Receiver, Jackal Say (rodeo), Shooterboy, Erasure Canto, What My Father Said In The Underworld (perfumes)

Sulfur Birth, Inferno, Leaderboy, Car Lot Leaderboy, Leaderboy In Love, She Play

To Asuncion

Williwaw Terror Pantoum

Dream Of Bones originally appeared as a broadside from Arundel Press (Los Angeles) and later (as translated by H.C. ten Berge) in *NRC/Handelsblad* (Netherlands)

From The Famine Catalogue (as translated by H.C. ten Berge) appeared in *De Gids* (Netherlands)

Terror Pantoum, Knives Wake, He Wire, NdjenFerno (excerpted) and Shooterboy appeared in *Raster* (Netherlands) as translated by H.C. ten Berge

Kill Series originally appeared as a deluxe limited edition book from Arundel Press (Los Angeles)

Published in the United States by Vatic Hum Press, San Francisco, California

ISBN 0-9654877-3-3

Contents

She Play

She play that throw your voice in the dead man game
She tamp her voice down deep outside herself
Pull from that frozen slant-front eat-hole slot
A baby I want you baby baby I want you
She coy her broken mouth and say she charmed
Slouch and spin the pistol cylinder
She narrow back into her throw-voice self
He say he want that crotch-lick candy game
She dick him in the mouth with the pistol point
Ask him how he like suck-gun roulette
He call her daddy's pop-tease sugar-slut
The gun make that little bomb in the melon noise
He nod once up and down like he agree
She back and forth her voice in a haywire stitch
Fill him like a bull-dog fills his bitch

NdjenFerno

for Paul Naylor

To exit domain a bomb wave a front of boundary sites
A man walk a street while random around him ignite
One wire-ankle rig like a seismic-tendon to a trigger
One wrapped in a rolling-doorway try to smother it

These flash-cards reconciled as drive-by-fires
Insurance frauds or missing bags of clothes
A writing buys a piece of the processing plant
Render whose nail-shoes sigh on cement and go up

The name-house has them somewhere in veneer
The blond elastic rain beneath the saw on the fuel-floor
A video-inoculated child immune from the fire-storm
Steers keyboard flames to a cornered matrix-man

How the fire-axe open his cartoon hands and heart
Each impulse-induced event on a binary switch
The blowing-away release a spasm of highlight

On a blackboard globe a child chalks countries in

How names go out at the ends of fire-wheels
So this we will call the land of face-on-fire
So this the land of torch-hands-tossing-coins
Land of migrants land of blisters
Rolling reign of hungers and hunt-engines
We have scored the cut-board gutters and are warm
Whose mouths are blood-mills
Richly adorned
Land of cellophane and land of chain
Land burdened of businesses
Of pelts and cross-purposes
Of organ-doors on the fronts of see-through men

In this series a man leave his hands as decoys on a lake
And the hands themselves are on their backs and quiet
A man make a separate weather in a warehouse
Another is so happy with her car she goes in her head
In this series a parasite enter the sleeping woman's anus
Soon lay eggs devour entire system

She prefer a limousine or nail-boutique

She herself has hollowed many out

Later she line up

A shop sells how you look in fifteen years in a photograph

Later she line up

A shop sells machine that records your life

You can play back and erase it as you please

Or splice an experience in if you have the coupons

Later over dinner she tell a man she love his mouth

She tell a man she like a summer cruise

The photo in her purse she keep to herself

He tell her miners in darkness miners without lights

He tell her fingers run vertebrae like white water boats

She thinks to herself he thinks of someone else

She play it back and erase him on the spot

Later she leave the restaurant by herself

Crossing a bridge she drop the photo in

When it hits the plastic water she ignites

See in the index under fuels made from ourselves

One whispers animal stories on the cheek of the wire child

One whispers over and over in the index of smooth pairs
One gone in a blast says bury outcome's icon
The stainless impact-voice-connector listens
Here in the seam the knife left are like horses over hills
Are like a blood rain are sapphire as blue only red
The seam the knife left in the cheek of the child
Says ribbons ribbons

If one against a wall in a wave of heat
If a person is seeking another is looking and looking
A person along the pavement churns in flames
Is it you is it you is it this one is it that one
In every house a blast has slammed its door
One says these shapes have shown themselves and gone
Whose lives were reefs the silence rests upon
One says the nations never sleep their swords
One says outside the room has triggered shields
Beneath the skin an inch or an even inch

If this were a children's book where clear picture-plates
Are laid over one another each with its layer of the picture

Whose question is what would it be had each never been
Whose question doubles each year like silver coins
Whose questions are sized for the boxes they will enter

Or the throne room of the third millennium
Everything in it made from fear-not and found
From foil and light bulbs from trash and discarded chairs
I was told to make it this way by the voice of God

Or the realm of hungry ghosts the realm of reaching
The smooth screen renders dice and investment choice
The laser printer purr as the options expire

If this were these but a page has lit itself in the deep past
Whereon were shown the connectors of words and things
Whereon entireties were made where none had been
One says stars before and one says set aside

She rises and bathes in the cool where the steam begins
She dreams a lustrous halo of her hair
She dreams the sideways chambers of her heart

Will right themselves

She believes herself a boat she believes the seas

Roll over on the pivots of their sleep

Several arrive in the late

Even through threshing knives

These elements reside in the rest of you

Plunge with you

Harmonic with your weight

Intent among desperate hands

Intent among versions of souls

In the underneath of tar

In the absolute underneath

When you identify the dead in the cave of coal

In the quiet in the tonnage in the index under eyes

When you hold the dead hands in your hands

In the tonnage in the quiet shouldering through

In the index under blast or gone-in-a-gale

When the dead ignite their names in your ears like flint

In the polished black of the permanent vertical walk

A chart of shatter-force falls through a lignite roof

It is said there are six worlds six veils six paper selves

When you see the dead hold their pasts in the tunnel-face

Bring a single voice bring rain some wheels of rain

You are one in an age of fissure-blades and teeth

A boat of broken sticks a boat of bronze a boat of flames

When you identify the dead you have passed the narrows

In the air in the falling cold you are in for a long climb

Erasure Canto

Then jamming mixed stained mauled

Shouting unsheathed

I cast that unwrapped speech down

Shattered outward

Golden with dark bearing

So that the voice gripping

Wave and tin dazzle

Knocked me cutting under my ankles

Like beasts and taking no bondage

I churned hyaline and heard

Singing howling fallen of voices

Upturned veins butt heart

Torn out all breaking and stripped

And I looked down struck and shuffling

That once untended in heart

Untended many things

And came changed different open unguarded

Told to stand

Prophecy

Enter alarm on a silent mechanical horse

Who says these lines in its head

We have gathered it all to one side like a wave in a box

And nothing unscalded stood

Whose ladders were dreamed into rungs as the feet advanced

Whose hands had held a mastery of reins

Enter the valves of exchange with their empty bowls

With acid-baths and pattern-racks on sides

Enter the past in its vibrant mechanical dress

The way it moves its hands so like the world

And enter the blind typhoon with its miles of mouth

How the radium-rings are halos over fists

It is play-back time in the box-seats of advice

Enter the portable values and enter the ice

Terror Pantoum

Around her death has been random all her life
Everyone a conscripted straw of history
So in her heart there are not innocents
Certainly the unconcerned are not innocent
Everyone a conscripted straw of history
Inanimate even before the bomb goes off
Certainly the unconcerned are not innocent
And she deplanes in Athens leaving the package behind
Inanimate even before the bomb goes off
Which is to say the subjects have done their final things
And she deplanes in Athens leaving the package behind
With terror the pivotal goes cloaked in the ordinary
Which is to say the subjects have done their final things
When the bomb goes off she is buying a tortoise-shell comb
With terror the pivotal goes cloaked in the ordinary
Her motives seem flat and secured as a folded knife
When the bomb goes off she is buying a tortoise-shell comb

So in her heart there are no innocents

Her motives seem flat and secured as a folded knife

Around her death has been random all her life

Receiver

Another person over here on fire taps wires
Though this is not my voice though
I am not one person here
Like a hotel fire I am not one screaming
Chop with your name
Chop with your working hand below the wrist
Who under fire within are tucked in fists
Of shelter after shelter in this series
Of floating paralysis of seeing directly
Who spoke a series of chains sealed with themselves
Like envelopes of ignition holding riders fire says
Each runner among each end is like stunned fingers
Braiding the bones of birds
It's called the upside down faces of the future
Receiver blinds a mirror
Feeds a fist of ashes down each throat
We are your blind selves they say
The scarcely anchored out-flares of the sun
Are not less sure

What wilderness totals columns wrought

Of breath or broken or boxed in combustion

Your heart its house of broken sticks

A braille of threshing ledgers where the fingers

Reading rapidly are fires along a river

Toward this anchorage of soot-bone-boats and ash

Of tonnage axe and lamp of digging out

In this series of boxed mouths

In this lake series in this combustion series

Loops of the torn transported through cipher blocks

In pages we carry who package painted windows

Onto murders rendered for purposes in this series

Of tongues and sets of opposing chairs

Whose dead are fixed as the gazes of flying knives

In antiseptic transport through this medium

Through this series of ornamental magics

In this riddle series in this rain series

Who under fire within are tucked in fists

Of hearts into metal roofs of shelter after shelter

Birth

Out it

Automatic

Into the virtual blood-box

Out it through the funnel

Of groin and moan

The primitive pushing out

Another and another

Into the silicon paw

The stress pulse and serum

Video game roulette and novocain

Stress-fix and matrix

Out put it

Into the replica

The strapped on goggle-scape

Strain it out

Muscle it out

Into the geo-digits

The engines

Into the disconnect

Asuncion

I abandoned my theory of rain   And my theory of the fulcrum   They are here
whose lungs sifted corpse-ash for air   I had searched for the magic language
of wakefulness   in the wind's rolling aviary of spent charge-carbons   Turn
off your voice   Every word is a government   listing toward overthrow
In flight I ditched the covenant of outcomes   Forward nothing

You will know siestas of motion and dust like the wings of moths   Murmurous
as aqua   Shank of ash   Tether of ash   Here the heat is durable as lust
The heart of the migrant bird is a cold hors d'oeuvre   Blue
like cracking smoke   A code toward your own   Like a plate
fallen on a floor of tiles   I wanted to witness the nuanceless   the evident

Mantle of bone   The wing is a blistered hinge without a door   Linear
as fast water   transformations indifferent as fire shoulder forward   Of your history
bring only your hands   Of bones the depth of rust   Of umber
buildings torn as reefs   The language surfaces sweet and muscular as rum
Of needles   As chalk   Not custom   Nor the great leap   No litmus   No litany

The light in the room is amber as a gull's eye   If something from memory opens
Everything aqua and broken the heart of   This candle   this one and this   Each death
the size of a silver dime   Rudder of bone   Clean as math   This blue cantina wall
among delicate flies   registers its mystery like a sheet of music   Even if only
the innocence of knives   Binary as hearts   Loomless   Fabric of parallels

I abandoned my theory of ash and my theory of innocence   Time's arrow
glistens past   Red oxide as west   Gradual as last   Begin   Begin again
Darker have   Erase   Nothing known   The last verb carries off the last noun
Awnings gust upward Heave rain   Unfasten upward   Let go the unlit   Rungless
as flight   Nothing toward   Nothing to put right   Far south   In Asuncion

Jackal Say

Jackal say jackal say jackal go jackal go

Guts like knots at a ro-de-o

Wear ’em ’round your neck like a bo-la O

Jackal say quick

Jackal say hide

Take your body on a buckaroo ride

Sew your mouth shut with a old cat hide

Where you gonna stick

Where you gonna ride

Jackal say world after world collide

Leaderboy

Leaderboy bait-sweet strolls among the sate-holes

He do that maskless grab-fandango dance

Scissor the glandular scent-scape ridden of poke

Leaderboy flash his nail-enamel luck

Parlay them back-pipe kisser-cogs on show

Their fawn-self parasite-parts obscured in styles

Leaderboy hole-hunt open-action-drive-train absolute

He ply that lawless viral inside war

He have that action on them all the time

Them pleasure-holes and money-holes complete

He know they cannot be guarded

When they open themselves to eat

From The Cutout box

Work the pieces until they separate sufficient

This is a death piece

Here the slot for it in this pretending to be a person

This piece pretend to know you

This piece walk and say nothing

This piece a weather piece

This piece pretend it is a school

These pretend to go

This piece a face like a stone this piece a pet

This piece a fire fit here on this floor face

This piece a pattern rack slot here

This piece a doctor here a heart phone

Several sound pieces fit the speak slot

This pistol slotted for the hand

This piece a special blue for your window

This piece pretend to look out and see for you

Serchenengenettes

Through The Great Imperilment

Known clerically as

"Our Age"

A dim asphaltine strata

Of Shackenmobilehome facilitators

Ply the bent upreachenthicket

Scoopandprice matica-grabenhindge

Motorette hand-motions

Through tense clapitta-voguenthrall

Apt ropenrouser-pictophants

Bobette and Shick shop credica-phone

Orderette outtootenhobbyette

Glastenparcels glammasaks

Stakkenitemdroves "Our future"

Airfastness "of" servicide

Slikt

Car Lot Leaderboy

A squat make a tentative toe-hold on the lot
Leaderboy sight it side-swipe swift and move
His heat-seek coils in a plastic survey mode
Leaderboy sidle the shag
Do a syrup-spurt at the hear-hole part
Make his fingers meat-fork wide and flash
Them eat-hole cutter-caps full-blind
Start that narrowing-caliper roller-talk
Cod begin to bridle and remorse
Leaderboy tack with a pout and reassure
Shimmy the wipe in a rust-white low-ride van
Gullet the hide with a cloy-clamp endocrine close
Pop a money-shunt on the pocket-purse
Suck it out like a egg-sack wasp on go
Leaderboy make a lip light grooming coo
Route the cob on exit into traffic
Smooth his hair back light and fresh as magic

He Wire

He wire the portable time bomb with his nails

Say: What cannot do good go up in flames Say:

Halves make lies Say: Lies make sleep

Say: After the bomb

All rise

Kill Series

for Grace and Billy McKay

I Last

I have returned from the lake of ritual paper boats

Each holding a candle

It was not the tide that pulled them underneath

It was not the wind

It was not the tide that broke their paper backs

It was our hands

II Dream Of Bones

In my dream of bones all the bones are lying down together

There is a field of bones a city of bones a sea of bones

In my dream of bones the broken vertebrae of the hanged

Rest like tongues in the mouths of those who judged them

There is a storm of bones there is a deluge of bones
In my dream of bones under the bones are the pages of every book
So every belief is holding up its portion of bones upon bones
Among the bones no motives no riches among the bones
No flags no histories no borders among the bones
In my dream of bones there is a language of bones
But not a word for “fire” nor one for “faith”
There is only the word for “final” and the word for “once”
Even the smallest bones of the ears remember these
These bones of our lovers these bones of the unborn
These warrior bones these murderer bones
In my dream of bones the bones said tell them this
That turning away or walking away
The torrent of bones at their backs
That turning away
Or walking away
The torrent of bones at their backs
There is a storm of bones there is a sea of bones
In my dream of bones all the bones are lying down together

III Knives Wake

Which porch would death choose

It could be any porch

It could be the corner of the map where monks immolate themselves

There is a platform stretched out like the head of a drum

There is the ocean which never tires

Which porch would death choose

Which doorway

It could be the doorway through which a man brings his bride

It could be words rising in the throat like cars in a funnel cloud

An experiment begins wherein the lungs are gradually collapsed

These dials and meters indicate the mix

This rest of knives this sleep of knives

High above the brilliant pebbles fall

These wakings of wanting to kill

It's everyday as glass

It's in our fingers

It's frozen in

IV Spokes Of The Siege Engine

Each open body disbelieve itself

Those tunnel mouths with tongues like thick rail ties

Each open stomach of spools like a sewing box

The open dead will always disbelieve

Thistles of wire clumped in their hands like keys

These watch each one fall mute in a black pool

Who taught the screams to nest in a box like bees

The channel watchers spoke as the bodies split

Spoke trains of judgments freighted with sport-scores and stocks

While people fell from the earth in front of them

V The Cost Of Each

Each kill was the cost of a flawless Fabergé egg

Though the bodies themselves were clumsy as metal sacks

There is a hard formula

Its numbers bend like bolts of cloth under blades

Choppers by remote

Nailers whose hammers ride radio waves

It asks the nose if blood is a silver bath

It asks the eyes

It asks the ears to climb the shredder's octave

It asks the tongue

It wants to know that its numbers are understood

This math of dice

It wants to know that your hands have had their bath

That your hearts reflect like polished silver fists

VI Kill Processing

The item is logged in

Sometimes a load makes nothing until the mouth

Immaculate robotics clean the teeth

Behind the tongue tube simple drops direct to the anus

All other organs harvest-auctioned

It is polished at the automatic teeth

At the mathematics

Sisterly

This commodity fluctuates in value

This particular is an average item

Not a white or Christian item

This kill is clean as the gloves of a majorette

VII Listen

If a scythe passes through shafts

If a fire goes about the business of breaking sticks

These are not falling where one alone falls

When the wind advances there are feet without legs

If this continues

All

How a ratchet begins a metronome

Drums the advancing breakage

Drums the broom of flies

Drums names like nails in the sea

I know only that ours are not hands manipulated by wires

Diligence at the gates

The inverted embrace of cold

Even that which is shattered

Is made of shapes

VIII From The Famine Catalogue

I see a prayer resting beside a severed ear

They do in fact rest one beside the other

The ear has things other than the prayer to deal with

And farther along in the chapter I see a tooth lodged in a careful red brick

I think the illustration wants to point out why not everyone sleeps well

Or over here is a cash flow accumulating internally beside a row of ribs

And the ribs themselves cage nothing now

In an Easter dress in a halo of ribbons

In a sack of grain in a combine of bullets

A hand tugs at the dress death wears carrying away the children

And the mouth says take me too

And the mouth says take any of us but these

And death over here in a small balloon of print says

You are well spoken but after all

You are only a mouth

IX Tenebrae

In the threshing in the volume firing through the machine
  many were never again

Of this communion
  of this witness whose lips are the blue of low flames

If sharpening subtracts here are the fallen
  sign of the spark land of edges

X Clairvoyant

Of these I have seen the shape
Speakers within the wrists
Mouths of the underneath
Knot knot knot knot knot knot knot
A man struck by lightning will become a finder of water if he lives

I have seen the shape of words from underneath

As in mountains the turbulence beneath the path if you place your ear

These say

Killers

The names will be as a bundle of needles in your throat

Of those that to you were lacerated things

You will learn each as in the eyes

Shearers of children

Severers

This thing here this heart your hands will cleave to mending

You will learn the names

You will learn them

Your hands will gather broken sticks

Your hands will fashion wreaths

XI Jackal Say

Brotherhood of blood raiments

Brotherhood of bones

Death's passive muzzle cores the crowded wind

Packers by select

How tendons and hungers tie us to the world

Death's perfect dime of density

Whose dwarf eclipse we move among ourselves

How many shadows walk the crowded wind

The torn internal voices resemble rain

We walkers under them

How paths of those we hunt have washed us white

If each are weights we drown

We walkers on water

We mules of death we packers by delight

The mountains are men without wives

How rivers tend them

But for ourselves

Walkers outside

No such

XII Walking In

In the distance an explosion tugs the wind

The shock will spread like ink in a water bowl

A veil imprinted with pictures brushes the face

It is a message whose words move around as one tries to read them

Each day some task or other is taken up

How the empty lake surface locks and unlocks its fingers

In the sweeping bath of fire the fulcrum stills and extends

It is the revelation of mending

That one can divide the water but cannot break it

Two Books

Partenski, Marianna: *Misperceptions Of Roulette Odds In Random Gun Play*: Actual case histories of poorly advised or ill-suited gun chamber strategies. Focus begins with simple statistical matrix but later expands to guns in drawers to guns in the hands of children to betting circles and private killing circles to how to tell from the eyes when the luck runs out.

Beamis, McCheznie: *A Potpourri Of Ancient Greeting Cards:* Lively anecdotes and color plates combine to form a tidy table book. An interest will be the stylishness of flowers. An interest will be holidays no longer here. Motifs wherein the subject has a laugh will be an interest. And to the dead in the old fashioned way. And to the sick with a bright little wish. And to one you have wronged and left upon the street. And to mother and to father and thank you for this and thank you for that and this for the first-born's first year and this for the child you have lost.

What My Father Said In The Underworld

He said knots in each and climbing

He said Bombay gin straight up in a cold cup

And: Wireless we walk

He said: I hurt myself on the straight line

He said: Power becomes your hands but not your eyes

And: The carriage of leaves will not have windows

Not so the innocent dusk with its rose-bunch and foil

When all the rocks are shouldered where they stand

He said each paints his own in a locket of ice

Wheel

If a wheel the size of a thimble rotates in the heart
Gold and adjusted to needles from years of use
If the turnings themselves are small as second hands
But cumulative so now they are seas
It is so on a path through a house of exquisite woods
It is so at the barrier reefs of lacquer and silk
How the words go around in their phonographic tracks
In the dark in the chill in the automatic space
Endless collisions backward into selves
Where the beach ran out at the stones of a distant point
Where youth collapsed in the eyes like a house of ash
Where a man with a glass of wine danced within a gale
If the names fly apart and the faces fly everywhere with them
And nothing returns like a fist full of rain in the sea
Each single light extinguished in the whole
On the mystery screen where the shadow persons battle and embrace
In the realm of phantoms joined in the realm of grace

What My Father Said In The Underworld

Perfumes intoxicants lead me

Cupped sensual anchorages into

Paper cutout replicas of selves

A storm of talk balloons at the siren-rocks

He said: All deeds are harbors in a row

All replicas

And the figures in them edged with toil and chance

He said the paper flags are passing foils

He said: My hands were flames in a paper world

The Method Of Steepest Descents

Where flux is some path in a heat plane

It begins this way

The weight of engines tearing off the wings

At a point of infinite products

She says: I am freight and have no hands

Them triggers on sides

Them outcomes under fire

Size me for it size my shoulders for it

From ignition the method shelters no reverse

Number me in it

Count the daylights in it

It does not begin like this it begins like this

I mean steep

I mean straight down

Leaderboy In Love

Leaderboy yoke him a she-sweet money-sock

He have a dazzle loose-knit way of talk

Goes: We got all the fluid drives in common Palmy Rump

Her earlier stick he haul behind and murder crisco-slick

Have his pant-hose on her in a jiff

Her hind he calls his heart-beast jellyette

Out loud he nicotine her yap-slot shut

Lose a finger up her semi-sweet

Piewaypoundapoundapound

He make things marvel

She tight her to him like a tattoo net

He drop her like a snizz-wipe two weeks wet

Hoorant

He-Ron Shtat Horedgeable Byndoseks
Runkt Edloodiary Plugnostable Horkt
Chalkstent Pindable Mirsoolean
Stednosteeary Ordanene Wyrent-Blungd

Coryannettalene Fost Andreeable Glistent
Hosticene Rahz-Mosstent Heh-Hykst
Dresofferynd Shez Bozenwentched Rikt
Bordshokt Butched Ekteckyaught Notcht

Hemalder Vytaskene Droze Peelaqur
Vorkshter Byte-Liggerscant-Fresht
Kutch-Wurmsholkter Frait Loobenmansk
Shoze-Rentchenscat Tee-Stikker-Tot Zu

Krenked-Mortenide Uxtox Tryonzenene
Shostable Hoorant Krocho-Emplozenmesh
Trybrandakle Hukt-Forentaskew Vikt
O-Tyde-Ron-Tyde O-Tyde-Ron-Tyde Krushkt

Shooterboy

Shooterboy drive him a skin-blue Belvedere

He keep his kill-shit crammed beneath the seat

A two-hole sawed-off kill-stick and a tarp

He carp-hunt up and down them kill-shit streets

Look for him some young ones freshly lost

Tap them dancey-barrels duet-style point blank

Tarp and toss the blood-bag in the trunk

He do that pout-date tar-pit ride-around

Sight him a sulky snow-faced candy-boy

Lick him a lolly-murmur dark as joy

Inferno

One sighs a stream of flame with a word at its end
Another goes altogether in a blast
A word that is oddly cold and without weight follows up
It is not beyond the stress-inoculation of the nerves
To know that these who are on fire have hearts
Consumed in our holdings
As hands themselves are burned
On the ropes of climbing and decline
It is not beyond what we could come to learn
In the bilge-gut and whore-wash of gathering
That these who are on fire
Have hearts
In the brute roulette of grabs
Straightforwardly they are fuels
In the mirror of inferno
One sees a figure on fire and turns away
Convinced it is someone else

Holders

Mine call them that watch it go into flames: "Holders". Who
stand in their furniture forms at the slaughter doors. Whose
ears are eels at the shifting radio-reefs. Whose eyes are
darkroom trays in the chemical cold. These call themselves:
"Bystanders". These call themselves: "Innocent". But mine
call them here in the mouth of fire a word on the Lick-Master's
tongue that watch it happen: "Holders". Because their days
are adornment plays in the prop-land of credit and cake.
Because their tacit tongues are terrorists. And none
would be on fire at all if these fucks had looked at their
hands and understood for a moment what they were for;
and reached through the broken glass and pulled someone out.

The Method Of Steepest Descents

It's hangers and bones it's sticks and stones

The weather is the handsome tarp of God

These sea bearings these under waves

Them one two three fingers under waves

And the ropes are all in the heads

And none in the hands

And the ladders out are all locked up in heads

Them wave runners them passers over

If miles were wakes like years are rakes

If tenuousness were tiles

She writes I am miles and miles and miles

She writes the good love their mistakes

Socket

It could begin by saying it is the land of instant-lenses clicking in rotation
It is the land of stunt-seeing and diagonal-discourse and eye-shadows and blocks
It is wavering a shrinkage-format-mapping that decoys the object-permanence of tongues
It is wavering a rapid-target-mask that coffins the triggered face in a photo-fit
Insatiable torpors of range-wire modulate the landing zones with fires and shot
Amazed and struck a column of file-sort-readers shunt and spindle coupon-premiums
Out and barrier-cold the purpose-wheels and strivings intravenous-as-fears extend
Screens and dosage-arrows forward through bearings tilted fists and easement-courts
Over bone-bricks and bone-breads fevers aside whose broken-hands and bankable-lives
Issue insufficiently for credit-brands and roller-trains of allocated fuels

Outages and voice-implants revolve expectant orbits over tonnage-ramps and looks
Sideways mirrorings jettison styling-reels through folder-skins and tanning-tiles
Outside a weapon ordinates itself in a lode of dice on a ball of tin and dancing
It is music it is parallel and muscular it lifts terrains it rivals the dense
Optimal ladderings-up it overreaches forging instantaneously brief devotions
Out of riddle-prayers and mystery-plays the rest a sensate shadow-pool in red
And ocean and gradualizations wildly marginal talent-cells pliant and for-sale

Formulate iconographic scripture-phones within whose pay-minute dial tones
Rosters of select magazine-anchorages trusted-by-the-stars and bridgeable
Incorporate their demographic sack-process vertically shuffling grab-and-budget
Workings in a hunt-and-luck-tube angular to instinct but popular by choice

If fire accepts the breath of a man in speech if lungs pull closed with the force
Of doors and clothes that walk through flames as words through blades if storms
Hollow their nascent richness transparently various and warm among fabulous agents
Worn as interior fabric-holds clear-through and inherent there falls a clear voice
Lavish in format and foreign as doors in the sea through which an arrow flying
Backwards from the heart entails and parts the sound-wall of want and mouths
For these are many and these are many more but a blind has trained its blackness
Into each and drives as down a coast extolled with nails and tune-boxes everywhere
Housings and tape-replicas of jammed order-lines through which item-plugs conduit
Poorly concocted debt-roulettes and volume-heated modules played over and over
Beyond which noise-windows shower additional generous mists and these taken
Initially though not at face presage that acreage of bounty and delight over
Whose cover of keenly negligent life extends an essential width and balance toward

It could say its beginning into the mouth of the brightly elastic surf it could
Elevate its cycle of bet-and-sweep across a dice of hives and swarm-song-reels

It could fold its destined horizon into pearls or demons into chrome or into flight
Or bind its feet in a twine of native pelts and celluloid to try the needle's strait
In a time of lucid dreaming in a time of cosmetic face in the dawn of knives
Whole mining starts torrential shovel-waves encoding porous rock-bits value-wise
And tonnage-wise whose ramps from earlier open load-lift-arms inside black-bags
And audit-trails through corner-blocks from which the market manages its levered
Tidal-wash across these many who have witnessed water-walls of unsound bricks
And lived scarce-boat and bail-boat and carried ungrounded forward in roiling
Whiteness among faces heavy as lodestones heaved by dam-breaks through cities
Of marvelous terraces and perfumed ices whose languages enamel classic postures
And wave a packaging plan at the passing drownage at the pulsing fury of hands
Because these though shred and throat-pulleys claw the underneaths for basic air
Are not reportable structurings from which an ample-return can make a crush
Like wine or the absolute color of wine or so much taken-in that those along
The banks reaching out their hands are knocked blunt where hearts and eyes were
Anvils are and a manufacturing noise that pulls utility from ore before
Children from white water and fashions jingles beside death-rattles and pitches
Beside tar-pits though its treaties with itself are tidy as codes and fencing

But the wind has broken its overhanging hands and the sea its hands below
And these from the weight alone of lies and dredge-mills buckle and rupture

Though this the blow-box fails anytime to say so sanitized are its plastic
See-through gloves and parceling-modes like fabulous surgical-lasers where whole
Organs are tugged from incisions the sizes of dimes and linear gene-bridges
Correlate the generational mix to fasten-out the lesser amplitudes of grasp
Where rigidly cleansed columns of motivationally-saturated team-combatants
Occlude intentionality favoring heavy-rousing and blanket-gearings while
Eager parental-circuits bubble and calibrate grade-and-snipe-set mannerisms
Openly over snack and job-track-initiation-bees whose shackle-moldings heave
And split the off-course and corrupt after which many congratulatory cheeses
Isolate themselves and motion backwardly one to the other as though in a reef-lock
But gathered like balance beams or broken into orchestrated halves through clips
And inculcated freeze-frame pallet-briefs against the languid options of raw heat
And opened teeth that course each equatorial slide-heap-populace in every round-ribbed
Chromium bullet-belt and lacquered boot for these we are clever about and indirect
As a cellar-door in a cyclone-game of seamless tearings-upward that are smooth
As the cellophane package-molds of amusement-guns hard-wired to battle-screens
Pursued beside a ticket-spit and trinket-cage wherein the player inserts a kill-read
Card from a sub-disk-deck implanted at elementary and queued for automatically
Progressing function-fits to transmission the subject up the want-and-production-curve
Of market-siphons suctioning ritualized locations through vanity-hoses and
Exchange-manifolds purporting intricate benefits but primarily imposing a stiff

Compendium of add-ons and worthless-without-which enhancements whose need-to-have
Switches fire automatically after the initial acquisition is brought into use
Across a static socio-normalization block where mouths shape openly self-invested
Syllable trains whose cargo is a mass of appetite and grab venues diced with various
Research probes and gloved couplings fast-forwarded through switch and tie routines
Whereunder fires erode the torturous grip of stilt and spasm shopping spree displays
Whose mannequin-sifted credit-quick device extends its fiber-optic currency-suck
Through rows of splayed accounting entry zones and item-spit demand delivery ducts

It could say its evenings webbed in silence and cargo it could say its evenings
Bent into the dark like a face from a fire it could say its margins of error
And erase itself like a sky it could say a north extends or a south begins
It could say the wires are words with wings or a west or a road of silk and dust
It could begin by writing a region on the under-arch of a dancer's half-bent foot
It could begin with an alphabet that folds its answers under like seas or sites
If a counting begins to lengthen like a silver strand in the heart or a reaching back
If a counting begins its echo of multiplication through a door of names and a door
Of rust an elaborate mapping sized for a single life ignites its path in a palm
In a reach in a rock on a harp by an opened stop in the notes or the wave of notes
Whose origins extend in a vibrant double of strings whose blue ellipse uplifts
Like a breath from a depth or far below and dense as essential white enclosed

At the socket windows every world is a part of the package plan at the socket windows
The raised vortex of item-banks and wants creates a primary weather of suction-zones
Whose artificial vacuum-loads implode the existing balance of want-and-withhold
In a transmitted house-to-house for hidden ore-beds of currency and loose change
Behind a cellophane wall from loot and hoard in the undertow how later it wants to
Talk about paying it back how later it teaches a special class called bust and revive
And spend and the churning streets and the rocket mist of frost and remote how the
Realm is titled performance and reward how the sign is an hourglass by an assay-scale

At the windows of clorox and nicorette at the windows of jade and tomorrow at the
Rotary versions of worlds at the splice-blade's teeth in the web of titanium sponge
On epoxy wings how the flight of the scythe is black on the back-lit screens
How it ends with a stone from space on collision course how it ends with the falling
Away of walls between notes on the blank terrain with the rupture of cause
And effect its persons auctioned in boxes a sack at their feet of their papers
Or night of sirens night of dice and stones at the turning away of the loop from the
Cut-glass gems at the windows of rearview archery and coke how the loom un-weaves
The tracery of home at the cross hairs of lust and cartoon on the frontage roads
That border nuclear winters in the silo of resonant pairs in opposing lines
In the carnival-zones of worship and remorse at the socket windows a woman displays

Herself beside burning cars and children gathering leather for making soup
At the socket windows panoramas of wildlife expose synthetic households in a soak
Of staged dramatic bits and outcomes at great expense intwined with actual footage
Spliced to conform to a scripted universe of pre-gauged queues and material prods
In the palm of the avalanche at the socket windows at the stress-mill-mouth at the
Windows washed with adrenaline and slush at the thigh of the chipper-blade in the
Hail of change how it handles a pocket-guide to the picture-parks below the luxury
Boxes of liquor and ice how it rolls the wayward into cigarettes at the pendulum hip
At the dock of hours at the wrist at the pivot of grasp in the socket walls

Files of life-facts exit open windows into fires files of every kind outlining
Every moment of lives exit on winds drawn out of windows by heat and into fires
The land extends its silent bath of ash its sunder of notes and news its hash
Of outcomes or a word aligns itself with an exit wound or a word accepts the weight
Of its travel plans or at birth a radio-ticket attached through a window of skin
At the shoulder blade machines a prize drawing later or later on a code is read
Into the eyes of what are the various values and measures for iced in their wreaths
Of ribs and heavy water whose tidal prolapses heave a procession of bar-code-kites
In a mock-up of the world as snug and priced on a register-string of raisinets
And chops or a plot is manufactured in a house where the furniture has worms
And will soon collapse or mouths in a dinner-box whose evenings of paired teeth

Allow them nearly to touch how things are killed as bars of steel are planed
Into finished rolls how arbitrary wires exact their cuts how things are killed
Where they stand in a rain of fraction-blades through a polished wrist on a canceled
Loin at rest and sculpted ice how things are killed across the curl of photographs
That blister in the heat these last of everything if each are hands that hold
A painted face these gone of all ages as if weeping and war were ground water
And ground cover as if horses were mercury heavy and fluid whose menders of distance
Were drums in a silver dirge of talk and bones that would match if it chose to hunt

If a shovel and a prayer meet voice to face in a place of deserted buildings
And abandoned cries beside galleries of staged sentiment crowded into appointed
Calendar-zones hoisted through memory ore-channels leached to a syrup of spent
Intent and fossilized response how vertical knives hold lists in their sides like lungs

How the ornamental wind brings smoke and wings if an exit begins to form in a woman's
Heart if an exit begins to form in the heat of a breath in the blind machinery
Of faith and form through which intrudes a sign or a series of signs how the engines
Accept the fuels into rotary claws how the motions are of hands in their piston forms

And eyes in the form of valuation-traps and pity-motors strapped to money-wheels
In customer-target-zones whose glamour-shots and time-lapse-nodes exude a scent

While each extracts its silver at the gate of rotating consultation fees in a box
Of interchanging family tubes on a binary track across from the cutting boards

If a place explains itself in a sack of shards if a place where feet struck locks
In the ground with their heals accelerates from an edge on a bed of wheels and loss
Where disarticulated conveyances scatter their marriage of severed hands and gears
Across an actinide field of mirror-works and pasts infolded into mileage and exhaust

If a mountain finds its place in the lake-moss floor if a head wind finds its house
If a drum is called a spoke in a fan of streets if a leash has kept a hand and
Throat apart how the sea in its cubic paragraphs of breadth cannot be known nor
The famous aluminum heart nor a voice below waves nor the infinite machinery of eyes

In its region of collectibles and tribes in its region of muffled drums across
Economies of scale in the inch-work of shattered glass at the depth-charged selves
If an un-bribed hand if an un-bought tongue if a cedar boat sets out under single sail
How the wind is a kind of wish-wheel on the levels of afterthought in the blue shift

In the world by inches these cargoes in the world by inches these names that are
Each one an inch on the light years of breath that carry each like fingers carry
Gloves how the prayer-holds bind the stainless in the theaters of saved-face

How the reliquary bones are bridgeboard knots on the climb straight up

In the church of the prolonged mortality chronically oxidized prayer-boxes
Articulate heavenly intentionalities outward over transiently scavenging sea-wash
And serially imbedded torque-residuals whose slotted family-zones now limited to frames
Implode their fractional grist through a chore-hole of tender marionettes and chits

Elsewhere portents of rescue resolve themselves in circular carbon sheaths
While portable dimmers rotate erratically calibrated power-sucks among speeches
And hooks work angularly upward through food-bait chains and service-first-facades
From which a delicate tracery of clasping incisor-springs fires grip-manifolds

Over predated cordiform postal-cuds whose spits revolve a cylinder court-roulette
And a mute-before-shackle code upon whose carriage of bones and pouting masks
A dozer shudders its crank-box leveler-blades and cleaves the white wave-face
With its shearing-oars whose hands absolve themselves in a bath of wine and groins

These waters work a nest of eraser-phones and closure-clamps across depleted
Memory codes and non-sequential grief-burst lotteries within whose odds and rigs
Are found a tangle of doors and a ribbon-map that runs its legend along fires
And lines along blue roads beside whose tongues are mouthed identical words

Or over here an intersecting thirst and a caliber-box propel an unhinged event
Through a dodge ball of pleading mouths and insistent barks that snap like props
And later the laid-out are coined in a roller-toss that handles their husks
Toward delivery zones of caffeinated parts and turning legend-lodes and sighs

Because to look as a concrete cube would look at the sea and not turn away
And to look not the way of a snapshot quip and serial word-cusp but to look
Directly with an edge as crisp as money and to look not through lenses but evenly
With ones own eyes and to reach toward and not away with ones hands and ones heart

Because collision embarks a paper-frame on a lake of dancing scissor-blades
And flames that hold the hinges of ankles like hungers among weathers and faces
That pass through unseen fingers like secret combinations of cards in a shuffle
Of this place whose cantilevered bridge-work-names emboss themselves on sleeves

If a blanket torn from the sea explodes through the coastal streets and breaks
Its woven net of salt and weight on a single house whose engines are fastened doors
So too will the hand-over-hand ascent on the rope of fire attached to the sky
Begin where the shock of a new blank space and unbuilt roof and wall begin

It could be the land of the plus and the land of the minus each and each and each

And each and each it could be the land of the zig-zag men and canyons and polished
Cars of the layers of doors from this to this and again or the sellers of hand-held
Pegs for the peg-board-climb or the archery of sympathetic looks it could hold its
Own in a ring of teeth and wires in a jazz of scars on the flecked linoleum floors
Or the mentionings of rivers into rocks like ice at the piercing of ears or myths
In the perfumes of pasts or the docket of tongues where the sums are brought to bear
Through the portages of alcohol and rain through the portages of silk and cyanide
A science explains how the world in entirely strings and barely bound how the soul
Is a spiraling stair like concertina wire in the forgery of light in the crazy glass
Of saints and commercial loans if an ear could gather back a scattered voice
Like a fist of pollen if an ear could pull the words from the wavelength air
And draw them up like flames to be understood as heat itself is understood on skin
It could be the land of the tabula rasa course-ways of bullet trains and blasting caps
Of the cult of the silver lining and money-back a science explains how the case-loads
Are handed down in the switch-back etching-plates of the bloodline's show-and-tell

And for such the rolling-leveler-blades expand their landscape-corrugation-zones
From elaborate rental-perches where mergers and acquisitions volley over nets
In a festive rotary of contained friction while farther-in a mill of concave
Mutterings rolls its mouth toward the blast-furnace-face beside which myriad
Shovel-holders heave the residual heart-peat into flames and yawn toward ratcheting

Ledgers of pay-scale-pegs and litigation-boards wherein the shadow-holders score
Hysterical-hierarchies of pleading batched from public-advancement muzzle-phones
Of ritualized praise and kneeling over stones if the sun melts a woman
If a tangle of bones by a calcified lake is deemed to be that of the redeemer
If a socket appears in the side of a waking voice if a socket arrives through which
Occurrences pulse without denomination on a jolt-and-mirror-curtain torn awake

If a watch extends its calendar-box to include the days of absolute ice and the days
Of drowning and the days of the lacerating of tongues and the heat of interior
Brandings it is so because the hands have made it so at our behest it is so
Because the kill-house card-and-gravity-shows extend their walls and locks because
The cost-contained-executors loitered on the margins of knife-works and did knots

In the palace of he-dog and spine he-demon have him a mechanical mouth or a mouth
With that mechanism in it say these automatic sounds say sectors say sections
It say the up and down game it say original memory how the lap-box have a door
From the carbon black with the one-way turnstile and the wall on the other side
Without a voice and the voice itself a kind of particle board for an inside house

In the land of genetic knitting in the land of slips in the place of octagonal dice
In the pounding place when the watchwords have passed the last lips when the eyes

Are coins when the passwords have watched the last lips in the rain of coins in the
Innings of fracture and run in the silver trace in the land of the fractional glimpse
In the pounding place when the hand-holds are fevers or sails on the pounding slate

A north extends its boreal dancing silks against the crush of imploded inks
In the absolute action of light within the choke of density and ice thrown wide
Through fields whose vertical acres expand against coils of coal outside the wedge
Of pockets and smoothed foils that line the interior walls of the finely boxed
In each this possible thing measureless explosive in grasp above each frozen reach
Each anchorage of wakefulness in each and each setting out from the shore of shreds
In each an anchorage calm in the rain of shreds and each setting out into breakers

About the Author

Lindsay Hill was born in San Francisco and is a graduate of Bard College. His previous books include *Avelaval* (Oyez) and *Archaeology* (Saint Lukes Press). Hill has worked in the investment business and, more recently, as a public housing volunteer.